SPORTS CARS

MOTOR Mania

by Sandy Donovan

Jan Lahtonen, consultant and safety engineer, auto mechanic,

and member of Porsche Club of America and Audi Club of America

Lerner Publications Company • Minneapolis

Copyright © 2007 by Sandy Donovan

Lerner Publications Company
A division of Lerner Publishing Group
241 First Avenue North
Minneapolis, MN 55401 U.S.A.

Website address: www.lernerbooks.com

Library of Congress Cataloging-in-Publication Data

Donovan, Sandy.
    Sports cars / by Sandy Donovan.
       p.   cm. — (Motor mania)
    Includes bibliographical references and index.
    ISBN-13: 978–0–8225–5928–3 (lib. bdg. : alk. paper)
    ISBN-10: 0–8225–5928–5 (lib. bdg. : alk. paper)
    1. Sports cars—Juvenile literature. I. Title.
  II. Series: Cars.
  TL236.D66 2007
  629.222'1—dc227   2006000268

Manufactured in the United States of America
1 2 3 4 5 6 – DP – 12 11 10 09 08 07

Contents

Introduction—What Is a Sports Car?   4

Chapter One—Sports Car History   6

Chapter Two—Sports Car Culture   26

Sports Car Gallery   38

Glossary   46

Bibliography   46

Further Reading   46

Websites   46

Index   47

Imagine two cars stopped at a red light. One car is big and roomy. It can fit a family of five comfortably. It has a small, quiet engine that you can barely hear.

The other car is a roadster—a small two-seater with a convertible roof that can be opened and closed. This car has a big, high-powered engine that often needs repairs. Even when the engine is running smoothly, it's noisy.

Who would want to own the second car? Actually, a lot of people would. That's because it's a sports car.

What exactly is a sports car? Some sports cars are very expensive "supercars" such as the Lamborghini Diablo. This $180,000 car is built for high performance. It can go extremely fast—nearly 200 miles (320 kilometers) per hour. It can handle turns at high speeds.

The Mazda MX-5 Miata is a different kind of sports car. This little roadster costs about $22,500. It doesn't go much faster than an average family car. So what do the Diablo and the Miata have in common? They both look cool. They are the kind of car a person wants to be seen in. Even more importantly, they're both fun to drive. And the thrill of driving is what sports cars are all about.

Italian sports carmaker Lamborghini introduced its Diablo *(left)* model in 1990. This ultrapowerful and ultraexpensive car can go from 0 to 60 miles (96 km) per hour in just over four seconds.

Chapter One

SPORTS CAR HISTORY

The 1896 Duryea *(below)* was built by the Duryea Motor Wagon Company, the first U.S. automaker.

Inventors first began making automobiles in the late 1800s. Early cars were noisy, unreliable, and dangerous. They had engines that often broke down. They were also hard to steer and stop. Accidents were common.

And yet the car craze caught on. Why? Because driving was fun. People enjoyed driving down the road with the wind in their hair—even if that wind was full of dirty car exhaust.

Before the 1800s had ended, people were holding automobile races. These races took place on country roads and city streets. Drivers enjoyed the thrill of high-speed driving. And thousands of people showed up to watch the fun.

People also enjoyed the novelty, or newness, of driving. Cars were rare in the very early 1900s. Carmakers built their cars by hand, one at a time. This was slow and expensive. It made cars too costly for most people to afford. Instead, automobiles were for adventurous people who had money to spare.

The Birth of the Sports Car

As the years passed, automakers found ways to build cars more efficiently. This made cars less expensive. Soon millions of people around the world owned cars. Meanwhile, car technology continued to develop. Automakers built more powerful and reliable engines. They designed

The affordable and reliable Model T Ford *(above)* first appeared in 1908. The car introduced the fun of driving to tens of millions of people around the world.

steadier steering systems and better braking systems. These changes allowed automakers to build faster and more exciting cars.

Racing was a great way to test new-car technology. Automakers brought their new machines to racetracks to see how their cars performed. The most famous racetrack in the United States is the Indianapolis Motor Speedway in Indianapolis, Indiana.

It was built in 1909. Racetracks also began appearing in European countries such as France, Great Britain, and Germany.

In 1911 American automaker Harry C. Stutz entered a new car in the very first Indianapolis 500. Stutz's car didn't win the 500-mile (805 km) race. But its unique design caught a lot of attention. Stutz's car was lower to the ground than most cars of the day. This allowed

Ray Harroun powers the Marmon Wasp down the straightaway during the first Indianapolis 500 race in 1911.

The Stutz Bearcat *(above)* was one of the first American sports cars.

it to hug the road better than taller cars. It also had a longer wheelbase. The wheelbase is the distance between the front and rear axles of the car. Stutz's design made his car steadier at high speeds.

Stutz's car was a hit. Soon after the race, he began producing a similar line of cars for everyday driving. The line included a roadster.

Like most automakers, Stutz kept making improvements to his cars.

In 1914 he introduced a new model of his roadster. Called the Stutz Bearcat, it was one of the earliest sports cars. It remains one of the most famous.

The Bearcat was very popular with young, thrill-seeking people. It was fun to drive because it was speedy. And because it was set low, it really hugged the ground. This helped it handle turns at high speeds without tipping over.

CANNONBALL'S RUN

The Stutz Bearcat earned worldwide fame in 1915 when it crossed the United States in record time. Driver Erwin G. "Cannonball" Baker (1882–1960) drove a Bearcat from San Diego, California, to New York City in just over 11 days.

A World of Sports Cars

Meanwhile, many European car companies were getting into the act. Some of the most famous sports car companies were born during the first half of the 1900s. The French company Bugatti began to earn fame with its unique cars. The Italian automaker Alfa Romeo also arrived on the scene. Many great British companies, including MG and Aston Martin, began making cars at this time.

Many of these new automakers focused on building race cars. The cars competed in races around Europe. Car companies earned fame by doing well at these events. One of the most famous European races was the 24 Hours of Le Mans in France. This 24-hour-long race was first held in 1923. Other famous sports car races of this period included the Brooklands Double 12, a set of two 12-hour races held in Great Britain. The Mille Miglia was a 1,000-mile (1,600 km) road race through Italy. The Targa Florio race was held each year on the island of Sicily in the Mediterranean Sea.

Racers speed along the banked (sloped) Brooklands Motor Course in England during the 1931 Brooklands Double 12 race. The course's banked pavement allowed the cars to roar through turns at full speed.

How an Internal Combustion Engine Works

Nearly all sports cars have internal combustion engines. These engines run on gasoline and use a four-stroke cycle *(right)* that burns a mixture of air and gas to power the car. These cycles take place thousands of times a minute inside a car engine. Sports cars have many different sizes of engines. They range from huge V12s (12 cylinders arranged in the shape of a V) to small four-cylinder engines.

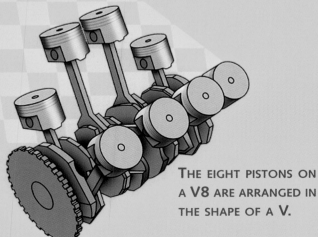

V8 ENGINE

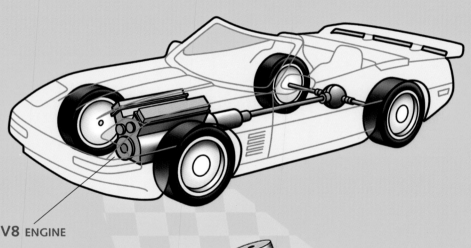

THE EIGHT PISTONS ON A V8 ARE ARRANGED IN THE SHAPE OF A V.

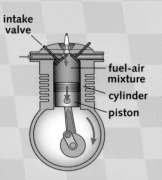

intake valve

fuel-air mixture

cylinder

piston

1. INTAKE STROKE
The piston moves down the cylinder and draws the fuel-air mixture into the cylinder through the intake valve.

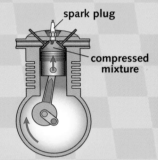

spark plug

compressed mixture

2. COMPRESSION STROKE
The piston moves up and compresses the fuel-air mixture. The spark plug ignites the mixture, creating combustion (burning).

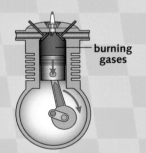

burning gases

3. POWER STROKE
The burning gases created by combustion push the piston downward. This gives the engine its power.

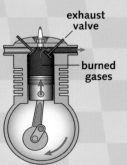

exhaust valve

burned gases

4. EXHAUST STROKE
The piston moves up again and pushes out the burned-out exhaust gases through the exhaust valve.

The 24 Hours of Le Mans

At Le Mans, France, the world's greatest endurance race is run on an 8-mile (12 km) course that includes country roads. The event is a huge challenge because cars must race for 24 hours. A team includes two or three drivers. Each driver takes a turn at the wheel. The race begins at 4:00 P.M. on Saturday. The car that has covered the longest distance by at 4:00 P.M. on Sunday is the winner.

Le Mans, early 1900s

Events like these drew thousands of people. The fans got a thrill watching the cars whiz past at 100 miles (160 km) per hour. After the race was over, fans still craved the excitement of high-speed driving. Getting around in a big, clunky car wasn't enough. These people wanted cars that were fast and fun to drive.

By the 1920s, many high-performance race cars weren't allowed on roads for everyday driving. They were too powerful and too hard to steer. Only trained race car drivers could drive them on such tracks as the Indianapolis Motor Speedway or the Le Mans course.

Stutz, MG, and many other companies saw the demand for fast cars. They created cars such as the Stutz Bearcat and the MG Midget. These machines were made to be part race car, part road car.

Rare Classics

Many of the world's most famous sports cars were built during the 1920s and 1930s. Most of these machines were wildly expensive. Like the very earliest cars, they were handcrafted. They were also very stylish.

Some of the most famous European sports cars of this time were the Bugatti Type 57, the Mercedes-Benz SSK from Germany, the Alfa Romeo 8C series, and the Squire from Great Britain.

Alfa Romeos, such as the one above, are among the most prized sports cars in the world. The powerful and elegant Mercedes-Benz SSK *(left)* was one of the greatest sports cars of the early 1900s.

These cars were long and low to the ground. They had powerful eight-cylinder engines that produced 150 horsepower or more.

In addition, many of these cars were supercharged or turbocharged. These devices forced extra air into the engine's cylinders. More air meant more fuel could be added too. The result was more power—and more speed.

Meanwhile, in the United States, a handful of companies were making sports cars. Like European machines, they were often rare and expensive. But American cars tended to be bigger and fancier. Some of the great American cars of this time were the Duesenberg SJ and the Auburn Speedster. The Auburn was famous for its unique boat-tail design.

The unusual rear end of the 1930s Auburn earned it the nickname boattail.

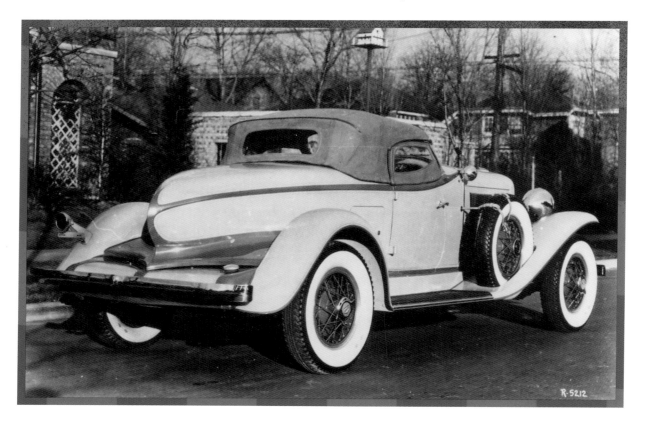

Prized Possessions

By the early 1930s, the Great Depression had hit Europe and the United States. Many businesses and banks failed. Millions of people lost their jobs, homes, and life savings. Only a small number of people had money to spend on such luxury items as sports cars. The really fancy cars such as Duesenbergs and Bugattis sold in very small numbers.

As the Great Depression continued through the 1930s, many automakers went out of business. But some started producing cheaper, more affordable sports cars. These machines didn't have huge, powerful engines or high-quality suspensions. But many of these cars, such as the MG M-Type, were still fun to drive.

Postwar Sports Cars

Very few cars were built during World War II (1939–1945). Instead, automakers built tanks, trucks, and other vehicles for the war effort.

Long, low, and shapely, the Bugatti Type 57 *(above)* was also very fast, thanks to its supercharged engine. During the 1930s, Bugattis were considered some of the finest cars in the world and have become highly prized collector's items.

Finding the Right Balance

Good balance is a must for a good sports car. A front-heavy car can be difficult to turn at high speeds. But too much weight in back can make the car's rear end slide out of control while turning. So car designers arrange the heaviest parts of the car to get the best balance possible. (The heaviest parts include the engine, the transmission, and the drivetrain—the parts that connect the transmission to the axle.)

REAR ENGINE, REAR-WHEEL DRIVE

PORSCHE 356

CHEVY CORVETTE

FRONT ENGINE, REAR-WHEEL DRIVE

Most sports cars, such as the Chevy Corvette, have a front-engine *(above)*, rear-wheel-drive layout. The car's engine is set toward the front of the car, and the engine drives the rear wheels.

Some cars—such as the Porsche 356—are rear-engine, rear-wheel-drive cars *(above)*. The Mini Cooper is an unusual sports car—a front-wheel-drive car with the engine in front. In the 1960s, Lamborghini experimented with a mid-engine layout. For the Miura, designers set the engine toward the center of the car, behind the passenger compartment. This provided excellent all-around balance. Most modern supercars have a mid-engine layout *(below)*.

McLaren F1

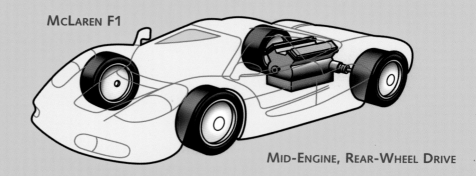

MID-ENGINE, REAR-WHEEL DRIVE

But the postwar years saw a rebirth of the car industry. The late 1940s and 1950s were an exciting time. Automakers created a wave of thrilling new cars with new designs and technology.

Some of these sports cars kept the long, low look of prewar vehicles. Cars such as the British Jaguar XK series had a long front end and a long wheelbase. But their fenders and overall shape are very rounded and streamlined. They are designed to cut through the air easily.

Automotive Geniuses

Both Enzo Ferrari (1898–1988) and Ferdinand Porsche (1875–1951) began their careers working for big car companies. Ferrari worked on and drove Alfa Romeo race cars. Porsche designed many of the greatest pre-World War II Mercedescars. He also designed the original famous VW Beetle of the 1930s.

The sweeping shape of the Jaguar XK 120 (left) caused a sensation when the car was introduced in 1948.

17

Introduced in the late 1940s, the Porsche 356 was the first car to carry the Porsche name. The rear-engine, rear-wheel drive car was fast and very fun to drive. It remains a popular choice for classic sports car collectors.

Meanwhile, some companies took the sports car idea in a different direction. In the late 1940s, German-Austrian carmaker Porsche came out with the popular 356 series. These were very small cars. Their four-cylinder engines were tiny compared to the engines in Ferraris and Jaguars. But the teardrop-shaped 356 was quick and nimble. It hugged the road in tight turns and was a thrill to drive.

As the 1950s rolled on, automakers worked to make the cars smaller and lighter. They designed smaller and more streamlined bodies. Cars such as the Ferrari Type 375 and the Jaguar D-Type were smaller than cars of earlier years. At the same time, some automakers were using bigger and more powerful engines. Both the Type 375 and the D-Type were stuffed with massive V12 engines that produced more than 250 horsepower. The mix of a lightweight car and a powerful engine made for serious speed. Both cars could travel at well over 100 miles (160 km) per hour.

Many other famous sports cars appeared in the 1950s. Some were low-priced machines such as the Triumph TR2 from Great Britain. This little roadster had a four-cylinder engine that produced about 90 horsepower. Other cars were all about high tech. The gorgeous Mercedes-Benz 300SL "Gullwing" was sleek and beautiful. The German sports car came with a high-performance engine that could top 160 miles (257 km) per hour. But its most stunning feature was its "gull-wing" doors, which opened upward like a bird raising its wings.

Meanwhile, U.S. carmakers didn't focus on sports cars as much. Most American cars of the time were bigger and heavier. Yet sports car racing grew in popularity in the United States.

The ultimate sports car of the 1950s was the Mercedes-Benz 300SL. The "gullwing" doors were a necessary invention to allow passengers to climb in and out over the car's high door sills. The vents behind the front wheels helped to cool the engine.

The 1951 Nash–Healey roadster *(below)* was the result of a joint effort between British sports carmaker Healey and U.S. automaker Nash–Kelvinator.

Organizations such as the Sports Car Club of America (SCCA) began to hold races around the country every weekend. Some of these events were held at old airports, such as the one in Sebring, Florida. Others took place in small towns such as Elkhart Lake, Wisconsin; Salinas, California; and Watkins Glen, New York.

As the sports car craze grew, tracks made just for racing began to appear. Some of these tracks, such as Sebring International Raceway and Watkins Glen International, still hold races.

Many American drivers liked small European sports cars. In fact, the small and nimble MG TC sold in large numbers during the postwar years. Looking to cash in on the trend, small U.S. automakers such as Nash, Hudson, and Studebaker began to make their own small sports cars. But these machines tended to be underpowered and slow.

Meanwhile, the most famous American sports car of all appeared. The Chevrolet Corvette was a small, sporty roadster when it first hit

The handsome Chevrolet Corvette *(right)* is by far the most well-known American sports car. This is a 1960 model.

Carroll Shelby

Carroll Shelby (born 1923) is a legend in the sports car world. The Texas native was a highly successful race car driver in the 1950s. After retiring from competition for health reasons, he turned to building high-performance sports cars. In 1965 Shelby *(top)* took a small sports car body from the British company AC and dropped a Ford V8 engine into it. The result was the blindingly fast AC Cobra *(bottom)*. The Cobra wiped out the competition in races for much of the 1960s. It is still a popular model with sports car drivers.

the streets in the 1950s. Over the years, Chevrolet has made many re-designs of its famous machine. The Corvette remains a favorite with sports car drivers.

Sports Cars of the 1960s

Perhaps the most popular design of the Corvette came out for 1963. With its pointy nose and gill-like slots on its side, the Corvette Sting Ray looked almost like a ray or a shark. Some models came with a massive V8 engine that could produce 400 horsepower or more.

Yet European sports carmakers continued to set the trends during the 1960s. Ferrari's 250 GT and 275 GT series mixed comfort and speed in a gorgeous package. *(GT* stands for *gran tourismo* in Italian. A "grand touring" car is designed to be both fast and comfortable.) They were also very expensive. By then Ferraris were thought of as the finest sports cars in the world.

The Lamborghini Miura *(top)* and Austin Mini Cooper *(bottom)* represent the range of sports cars that were built in the 1960s. The Miura was an elegant, high-priced, mid-engine supercar. The front-engine, front-wheel-drive Mini Cooper was fast, affordable, and great for everyday driving.

In the early 1960s, a new Italian sports car company rose to challenge Ferrari. Lamborghini made the GT 350 and the Miura. They were beautiful, glamorous, and extremely fast. They were equipped with huge V12 engines. Like Ferraris, they were handmade and very expensive. Only the very rich could afford them. These supercars were symbols of wealth.

Meanwhile, other automakers were building smaller sports cars. One exciting—and unusual—sports car from the 1960s was the Austin Mini Cooper from Britain. Tiny and box-shaped, the Mini Cooper didn't look fast. But it was lightweight. It was a front-wheel-drive car. Most of the weight of the engine, transmission, and axle was directly over the front tires. This gave the Mini Cooper fantastic traction and helped it stay glued to the road at high speeds. The Cooper earned fame by winning dozens of races in the 1960s. The car beat more expensive Porsches, Ferraris, and others on tracks where traction was more important than straight-line speed.

Sports Cars
of the 1970s and 1980s

World political events led to a series of gas shortages in the United States in the 1970s. Gas became scarce, and gas prices went through the roof. New government laws that called for safer cars also affected the sports car market. High-performance engines became rare, and small speedy cars were thought to be unsafe. But the 1970s did see some sports car success stories. For example, the Japanese Datsun 240 Z was very popular. It had a nice mix of speed and fuel efficiency.

Meanwhile, the leading sports car companies such as Ferrari and Lamborghini came out with spectacular new cars for the 1970s. The Lamborghini Countach was totally unique. It had a sharp, sloping shape and gullwing doors. The Countach's massive V12 engine was set near the center of the car. This gave the car very good balance in turns. And the Countach was unbelievably fast. It could top 185 miles (298 km) per hour.

The outrageous Lamborghini Countach caused a sensation when it first appeared in 1974. More than 30 years later, the 185 mile-per-hour (298 km-per-hour) supercar still looks futuristic.

The classic MGB *(top)* is a popular and affordable roadster. The fast and nimble rear-engine, rear-wheel-drive Porsche 911 *(below)* is one of the most popular sports cars of all time.

Few cars could challenge the Countach for speed and performance. But Ferrari's Berlinetta Boxer was one of them. Introduced in the early 1970s, this car could reach speeds over 170 miles (274 km) per hour.

But these supercars were just a few of many great sports cars built in the 1970s and 1980s. The Porsche 911, BMW M3, and Aston Martin V8 also had plenty of speed. But these cars didn't cost a fortune. Even more affordable sports cars of this time included the Mazda RX-7 and the MG MGB.

Sports Cars Everywhere: The 1990s and 2000s

The 1990s were good times for many Americans. The country's economy did well, and people had money to spend. Many chose to spend their money on fun and exciting cars. Nifty machines such as the BMW Z3 roadster and the Mercedes-Benz SL class appeared in more and more American garages.

In the mid-2000s, nearly every auto-maker produces at least one model of sports car. They range from the afford-able Mazda Miata roadster to the newest Lamborghini, the Gallardo.

U.S. automakers have also hit the road with their own new sports car designs. Some are mid-priced cars, such as the flashy Chrysler Crossfire and the ever-popular Chevrolet Corvette.

At the top of the heap are the supercars, such as Ford's new 500- horsepower GT and the wild 1,000- horsepower, 250-mile-per-hour (400 km/hr) Bugatti Veyron.

There are so many choices available. Sports car lovers have an exciting road ahead of them.

The $1.2 million 2006 Bugatti Veyron is the fastest road car ever built. This stunning machine has a massive W16 engine (16 cylinders arranged in the shape of a W, like two V8s attached side by side). The W16 produces a whopping 1,000 horsepower.

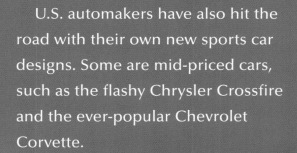

Sports Car Culture

From pint-sized roadsters to high-tech supercars, sports cars are made for just about every kind of driver. Some people buy sports cars just for looks. They don't really care how they perform. For others, speed and handling are the most important things.

You don't need to own a sports car to enjoy these amazing vehicles. A person can learn about them from books and magazines. Hundreds of great sports car books have been published over the years. Most feature great photos and cover the history and designs of the world's most exciting road cars. Popular car magazines include *Sports Car International, Road and Track, Car and Driver,* and *Motor Trend.* These publications include stories about new and old cars.

Car Shows and Performance Driving Schools

Another great way to enjoy sports cars is to go to car shows. Such events usually feature dozens or hundreds of cars on display. They give car fans a chance to see their favorite machines up close. Car museums can be found all over the country. Places such as the Petersen Automotive Museum in Los Angeles, California, feature sports cars from the past. Visitors can check out the cars, learn about them, and even buy books about their favorites.

But just looking at cars isn't enough for some. For these people, performance driving schools are the way to get the most out of their cars.

Classic car shows *(above)* feature machines from the past. The car shown above is a 1960s Shelby Cobra.

Drivers compete at Le Mans, France. The yellow car in the lead is a prototype. The two red Ferraris to the right are GT-class cars.

These are places where drivers can test out their cars on real racetracks. They can learn race car driving skills from the pros while having a blast behind the wheel. Most of these schools are quite expensive, but they make memories that last a lifetime. The most talented students can even train and qualify to become real sports car racers with the Sports Car Club of America (SCCA). The SCCA is a group that organizes sports car races throughout the United States.

Professional Sports Car Racing

Sports car racing is a very popular sport. The 24 Hours of Le Mans is one of the world's top sporting events. Le Mans and many other races like it are known as endurance races. They are about more than just going fast. To

Vanina Ickx, Racer

Belgian-born racer Vanina Ickx (born 1975) *(at right in front of her prototype race car at Le Mans)* is a very popular and successful race car driver. The daughter of six-time Le Mans winner Jackie Ickx, Vanina has followed in her father's footsteps. She has competed at the 24 Hours of Le Mans, in the Le Mans Series, and in many other racing competitions.

win, cars have to be able to endure, or last, driving at high speeds for long periods of time. Endurance racing series are popular around the world. In North America, the American Le Mans Series and the Rolex Sports Car Series hold races in the United States and Canada. The Le Mans Series is a similar set of races held on tracks in Europe. Both include several different classes of cars. The top classes of cars are known as LM (Le Mans) P1 and P2 (for prototype). They look nothing like regular road cars. Prototypes—specially built cars—are very low and streamlined. They are extremely fast. The GT classes of cars look similar to road vehicles. GT cars have some modifications to make them faster and safer for racing.

Rally Racing and Rallying

Rallies take place on public roads blocked off for racing. Drivers can compete in many different kinds of rallies. They include professional World Rally Championship (WRC) races and small SCCA amateur (nonprofessional) rallies.

WRC races are some of the most watched sporting events in the world.

Teams include a driver and a codriver. They race in specially modified sports cars on some of the toughest, bumpiest roads in the world. WRC events take place in 16 different countries. Teams race in all sorts of weather conditions—from the desert heat of Mexico to the snowy mountains of Sweden.

A Mitsubishi Lancer rally car bursts through shallow water during a World Rally Championship stage in Mexico. Automakers from around the world build and sponsor cars to compete in this famous event.

The Ford GT40: An American Supercar

In the early 1960s, Henry Ford II, the head of Ford Motor Company, tried to purchase Ferrari. The Italian company backed out of the deal at the last minute. So Ford decided to punish Ferrari by beating the Italians on the racetrack. Ford invested millions of dollars to produce a car that would whip Ferrari at the 24 Hours of Le Mans. The result was the Ford GT40, one of the world's most famous supercars. The low streamlined, mid-engine monsters finished first, second, and third at the 1966 Le Mans race *(below)*. They won again the following year. In 2005 Ford began making a new version of the car for normal road use. The stunning $150,000 GT is one of a rare handful of American supercars.

Two-time World Rally champion Sébastien Loeb of France slides his Citroën Xsara rally car through a turn during the Rally of Japan stage of the 2005 World Rally Championship.

THE DAKAR RALLY

The Dakar Rally is probably the most famous rally race in the world. The competition includes both motorcycles and rally cars racing from Lisbon, Portugal, to Dakar, Senegal, on the west coast of Africa. As with all rallies, the Dakar is a time trial competition (race against the clock).

A rally is a series of races, or stages, that take place over several days or weeks. Teams don't compete against one another to see who reaches the finish line first. Instead, there are time trials. Teams start separately (usually two minutes apart) and race against the clock. The car that completes the stage in the shortest amount of time is the winner. Spectators line the course to watch the brightly painted cars zip past.

WRC rally races are major events that draw hundreds of thousands of fans. But many smaller rallies take place all over the world. These races are often made up of amateur drivers who are racing for fun not money.

The SCCA holds hundreds of these rallies each year in the United States. These races are usually more about control than speed. The rally organizers create a very detailed map for the race. They also write instructions about where cars should turn and how fast they should go. The key is to follow the instructions as closely as possible.

The codriver helps the driver to follow the instructions as exactly as possible. This includes making sure the driver is driving at the average speed. To measure the speed, the navigator uses a stopwatch and a special calculator. The average speeds are always below the legal speed limit. Any team that drives faster than the legal speed limit is automatically out of the race.

Rally routes include several stopping places called checkpoints. Rally workers are stationed at the checkpoints. They score each car as it passes. The scores are based on how well the driving team is following instructions. The team must always follow the

Sports Cars on TV

The Speed Channel broadcasts many kinds of sports car racing and other sports car shows. On this channel, you can watch the World Rally Championship, the American Le Mans Series, as well as shows about the history of famous sports cars.

instructions closely in order to get the highest scores at the checkpoints. The team with the most points wins.

A lone car speeds through the desert of North Africa during the 2005 Dakar Rally.

This autocross competitor makes a tight turn in his BMW M3.

Gymkhana (Autocross)

Gymkhana means "athletic contest" in the Indian language of Hindi. In the 1800s, British citizens living in India held horseback riding competitions called gymkhanas. In the 1950s, American drivers began holding their own kinds of gymkhanas. But they were driving competitions that took place in parking lots. Control is the key. Drivers start, turn, park, back up, and stop. And they do it all in a small area and at low speeds.

In the early 2000s, a gymkhana is called an autocross competition. These events take place in parking

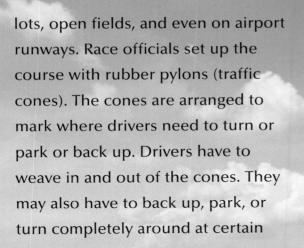

lots, open fields, and even on airport runways. Race officials set up the course with rubber pylons (traffic cones). The cones are arranged to mark where drivers need to turn or park or back up. Drivers have to weave in and out of the cones. They may also have to back up, park, or turn completely around at certain spots. The idea is to complete the course in the fastest possible time while not touching any of the cones.

Sports car fans young and old can always find a way to enjoy their hobby. And with new and exciting cars coming out every year, sports cars will be an exciting pastime for many years.

The thrill of driving on the open road is what sports cars are all about.

Suspension Systems

The suspension is the system of springs, shock absorbers, and other parts that connect the wheels to a car. The suspension has many jobs. It supports the weight of the car and keeps passengers comfortable by absorbing bumps in the road. The suspension also helps the car to grip the road by keeping the best contact between the tire and the road surface during braking and turns. To do this, the suspension keeps the car balanced as its weight shifts. For example, when a driver is making a hard left turn, the car's speed will shift much of the car's weight to the right. The suspension absorbs some of the weight change while keeping the tires in contact with the road to keep the car steady.

Suspensions can be "soft," "firm," or anywhere in between. Soft suspensions are great at absorbing bumps and providing a smooth ride. They are often found on luxury cars. Most sports cars have firmer suspensions. Firmer suspensions aren't great at absorbing bumps. But they keep the car from bouncing or swaying during high-speed turns.

Sharp turns are the toughest test of a car's suspension system.

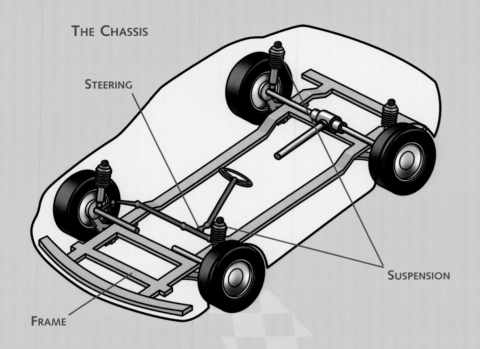

THE CHASSIS

STEERING

FRAME

SUSPENSION

The suspension is one part of a car's chassis—the basic underbody structure of a car. The chassis includes the frame, steering system, and tires and wheels.

Many different kinds of suspension systems are available on sports cars. Some are very simple and basic. Others are very complicated and high-tech. The most popular kind of suspension is the MacPherson strut system *(right)*. This simple, compact system was developed in 1947 by General Motors engineer Earle S. MacPherson.

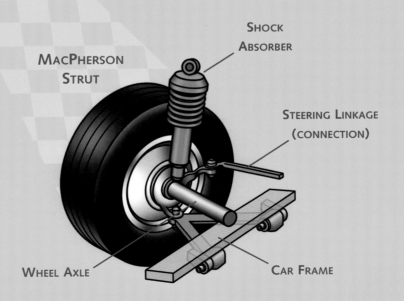

MACPHERSON STRUT

SHOCK ABSORBER

STEERING LINKAGE (CONNECTION)

WHEEL AXLE

CAR FRAME

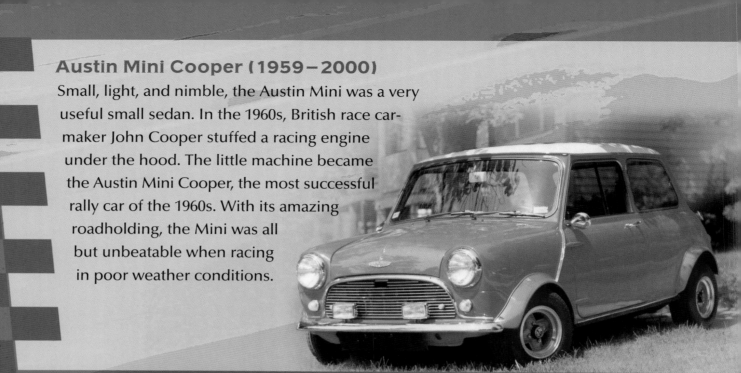

Austin Mini Cooper (1959–2000)

Small, light, and nimble, the Austin Mini was a very useful small sedan. In the 1960s, British race car-maker John Cooper stuffed a racing engine under the hood. The little machine became the Austin Mini Cooper, the most successful rally car of the 1960s. With its amazing roadholding, the Mini was all but unbeatable when racing in poor weather conditions.

Mini Cooper (2000–)

In 2002 BMW launched a new, updated version of the Mini Cooper to worldwide praise. Stylish as well as swift, the new machine was an instant smash hit with the public. The Mini Cooper S model *(right)* features a supercharged engine and wide high-performance tires. Note the placement of the wheels at the extreme edge of each corner of the car. This is a key to the Mini's excellent traction.

BMW M3 (2003)

The M3 is a specially modified high-performance version of BMW's popular 3 series two-door coupes. M3s are equipped with a powerful six-cylinder engine, high-performance suspension and brakes, and many other racing features. This car has been outfitted for racing.

BMW Z4 (2006)

BMW's latest roadster features cutting-edge styling and a powerful six-cylinder engine. Like the best modern sports cars, the Z4 uses high-tech equipment to get the best performance possible. This includes a traction control system. The system automatically adds or reduces power to the wheels to keep the car from slipping or spinning.

Chevrolet Corvette Sting Ray (1963–1967)

The dazzling Corvette Sting Ray of the mid-1960s might be the greatest American sports car ever made. With jaw-dropping good looks and a powerful engine, the car had everything. The machine proved to be a huge hit. Chevrolet struggled to build them fast enough to meet demand.

Chevrolet Corvette (2000)

Chevrolet has sold more than one million Corvettes since 1953. The car has been redesigned and restyled several times. The sweeping 2000 model shown here is the C5, or fifth generation, Corvette. A new C6 was introduced in 2005.

Ferrari Dino (1972)

Enzo Ferrari named this automotive masterpiece after his beloved son, Dino, who died of liver disease. Curvy, aerodynamic, and extremely fast, the mid-engine Dino was one of the finest sports cars built in the 1970s. It remains a hot collector's item.

Enzo Ferrari (2003)

Named after the company's founder, Ferrari made only 400 of these incredible mid-engine supercars. The Enzo's body is made of carbon fiber. This is a very light but incredibly strong material used on Formula One race cars and military aircraft. The car can go from 0 to 60 miles (96 km) per hour in just over three seconds.

Ford GT (2005)

The Ford GT40 earned its fame by dominating Le Mans during the late 1960s. The GT40 has been out of production for decades. But it has remained one of the most talked-about sports cars of all time. In 2005 Ford decided to honor the original GT40 by creating an updated version of the car. The result was the gorgeous $150,000, 500-horsepower Ford GT *(right)*.

Jaguar SS 100 (1936–1940)

The elegant Jaguar SS 100 was one of the fastest and most beautiful cars of the 1930s. This ultrarare machine (just over 300 were built) was one of the must-have cars among wealthy collectors of the time. Later models of the car were able to reach 100 miles (161 km) per hour. It was one of the fastest road cars of the day.

Lamborghini Murcielago (2002–)

Lamborghini named its newest supercar after a famous fighting bull. This powerful mid-engine machine features scissor-opening doors and carbon-fiber body panels. The car also has a special rear spoiler wing that adjusts as the car speeds up. As the car goes faster, the wing changes its position to keep the car firmly glued to the road.

Mazda MX-5 (1989–)

The Mazda MX-5 Miata is the world's most popular sports car. Mazda has sold more than 720,000 of these cute and nimble machines since 1989. Sold as the Miata in the United States, the third-generation (2006) model is simply known as the MX-5. The speedy roadster is highly popular with amateur racers. Hundreds of Miata races are held at tracks around the country each year.

McLaren F1 (1992–1997)

McLaren is best known for its success in auto racing. The team has won numerous Formula One World Championships. In the 1990s, the company put its racing experience into building one of the world's fastest supercars, the F1. The mid-engine car has an unusual passenger layout. The driver sits in the middle of the car for the best possible balance. The F1 at right is shown competing at the 24 Hours of Le Mans in 1996.

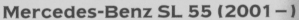

Mercedes-Benz SL 55 (2001–)

The SL (Sport Light) 55 is the latest in a long line of beautiful Mercedes sports cars. This sleek front-engine, rear-drive roadster features a powerful supercharged V8 engine. It produces nearly 500 horsepower. The SL 55 can go from 0 to 60 miles (96 km) per hour in just 4.5 seconds.

Squire (1935–1936)

The Squire is one of the more interesting stories of sports car history. Adrian Squire of Great Britain founded the company in the mid-1930s. The small company built just seven of these impressive vehicles before going out of business. Each one is a highly prized collector's item. During World War II, Squire worked for British aircraft maker Bristol. He was killed during a German bombing raid.

Triumph TR2 (1953–1955)

Sporty roadsters were all the rage in the late 1940s and 1950s. British automaker Triumph offered one of the best affordable roadsters, the TR2. Simple but attractive, the TR2 was not the fastest car of its time. With its 90-horsepower engine, the car had a top speed of just 107 miles (172 km) per hour. But the car was still fun to drive and was very popular in the United States.

Glossary

autocross: events in which drivers test their driving skills on an obstacle course

exhaust: hot gases created by the explosions that take place in an internal combustion engine

gymkhana: a sports car contest, often held in parking lots, that test drivers' starting, stopping, turning, and parking skills

horsepower: a unit used to measure an engine's power

prototype: in motor racing, a car specially built for racing

rally: a sports car contest held on closed-off public roads instead of racetracks

roadster: an open, two-seater style of sports car

suspension: the parts of a car that support its weight and attach its wheels

time trial: a racing event in which drivers race against the clock instead of one another

transmission: the sets of gears that transmit power from a car's engine to its wheels

V8: an eight-cylinder engine in which the cylinders are set in the shape of a V

wheelbase: the distance between the front and rear axles of a vehicle

Bibliography

Cheetham, Craig, ed. *Sports Cars: High Performance Machines*. New York: Barnes and Noble Books, 2003.

Lawrence, Mike. *A to Z of Sports Cars since 1945*. Bideford, UK: Bay View Books, 1991.

Marchet, Jean-Francois. *Lamborghini Countach*. London: Osprey Publishing, 1988.

Noakes, Andrew. *The Ultimate History of the Sports Car*. New York: Barnes and Noble Books, 2005.

Willson, Quentin. *Ultimate Sports Cars*. New York: DK Publishing, 1991.

McKenna, A. T. *Lamborghini*. Minneapolis: Abdo & Daughters Publishing, 2001.

Piehl, Janet. *Formula One Race Cars*. Minneapolis: Lerner Publications Company, 2007.

Raby, Philip. *Racing Cars*. Minneapolis: LernerSports, 1999.

Further Reading

Braun, Eric. *Hot Rods*. Minneapolis: Lerner Publications Company, 2007.

Doeden, Matt. *Stock Cars*. Minneapolis: Lerner Publications Company, 2007.

Johnstone, Michael. *NASCAR*. Minneapolis: Lerner Publications Company, 2007.

Lamm, John. *Supercars*. Osceola, WI: Motorbooks International, 2001.

Lee, Stacy. *Ferrari*. Vero Beach, FL: Rourke Publishing, 2004.

Websites

Ferrari World: Official Ferrari Website
http://www.ferrariworld.com/FWorld/fw/index.jsp
Learn more about the world's most famous sports car company from its official website.

Lamborghini.com
http://www.lamborghini.com/
Visit the official website of the Italian supercar maker to learn more about the company's history and cars.

The Sports Car Club of America
www.scca.org
Visit the Sports Car Club of America's website to find information about rallies, Solo II, and pro racing events taking place near you.

Index

AC Cobra (Shelby Cobra), 21, 27

Alfa Romeo, 10, 13, 17

American Le Mans Series, 29, 33

Auburn "boattail," 14

Austin Mini Cooper, 22, 38

autocross, 34, 35

BMW Mini Cooper, 38

BMW M3, 24, 34, 39

Brooklands Double 12 race, 10

Bugatti, 10, 25

Bugatti Type 57, 13, 15

Bugatti Veyron, 25

Chevrolet Corvette, 16, 20, 21, 25, 40

Dakar Rally, 32, 33

Datsun 240 Z, 23

diagrams, 11, 16, 37

Duesenberg, 14, 15

Duryea Motor Wagon Company, 6

1896 Duryea, 6

Enzo Ferrari (car), 41

Ferrari, 17, 18, 21, 22, 24, 41

Ferrari, Enzo (automaker), 17

Ford GT, 12, 25, 31, 42

Ford GT40, 31, 42

Ford Model T, 7

GT (gran tourismo), 21

GT racing cars, 28

Harroun, Ray, 8

Ickx, Vanina, 29

Indianapolis 500 race, 8

internal combustion engine, 11

Jaguar, 17, 18, 42

Lamborghini (automaker), 4, 5, 16, 22, 23, 43

Lamborghini Countach, 23

Lamborghini Diablo, 4, 5

Lamborghini Miura, 16, 22

Lamborghini Murcielago, 2, 43

Le Mans Series, 29

Marmon Wasp, 8

Mazda MX-5 (Miata), 4, 24, 43

McLaren F1, 16, 44

Mercedes-Benz, 13, 19, 24, 44

Mercedes-Benz SL55, 44

Mercedes-Benz 300SL Gullwing, 19

MG, 10, 15, 20, 24

MGB, 24

Mille Miglia, 10

Nash-Healey roadster, 20

Petersen Automotive Museum, 27

Porsche, 16, 17, 18, 24

Porsche 356, 16, 18

prototypes, 29

rallying, 30, 32, 33

rally racing, 30

roadster: description of, 4; examples of, 9, 19, 20, 24, 39, 43–45

Shelby, Carroll, 21

Solo. See autocross

Sports Car Club of America (SCCA), 20, 28, 30, 34

sports cars: description of, 4; origins of, 9; suspensions on, 36

Squire, 13, 45

Stutz, Harry C., 8–9

Stutz Bearcat, 9, 13

supercar: definition of, 22; examples of, 22, 23, 25, 41, 42, 43, 44

supercharger, 14, 15

suspension systems, 36–37

Targa Floria race, 10

Triumph TR2, 19, 45

turbocharger, 14

24 Hours of Le Mans, 10, 11, 28, 29, 31, 44

World Rally Championship, 30, 32, 33

About the Author

Sandy Donovan has written more than a dozen books for children on a wide variety of subjects. She lives in Minneapolis.

About the Consultant

Jan Lahtonen is a safety engineer, auto mechanic, and lifelong automobile enthusiast.